C000089657

HARRY COC

The Florence Duck Store

Poems from Italy

THE FLORENTINE / *Press*

HARRY COCHRANE

The Florence Duck Store

Poems from Italy

ISBN 978-88-97696-22-3

First edition: February 2021

All rights reserved | *Riproduzione vietata*

2021 B'Gruppo srl, Prato

Imprint | *Collana*: The Florentine Press

www.theflorentinepress.com

layout, illustrations and cover design: Leo Cardini | flod.it

No part or this book may be reproduced or transmitted in any form or by any means, electronic or mechanical, including photocopying, recording or by any information storage and retrieval system, without the written permission of the publisher and the author.

Nessuna parte di questa pubblicazione può essere riprodotta in alcuna forma o con alcun mezzo, grafico, elettronico o meccanico, includendo fotocopie, registrazioni, riproduzioni, o sistemi di archivazione e recupero dati, senza il consenso scritto dell'editore e dell'autore.

The Poems

SMS

i. m. Seamus Heaney

It was just in front of Nicodemus –
a self-portrait from Michelangelo
say art historians – and Christ below
wasted with the effort to redeem us

that the text pressed itself against my thigh.
What a cliché to say that my blood froze
and I could compose myself to compose
neither expostulation nor reply,

only this sonnet thirty-two weeks on:
yet another conceived in Florence
and mine to keep my hands off now you're gone,

a thanker of heaven for small mercies
and a tributary paying into torrents
of tributes, elegies, of sweet, smooth verses.

- 2014

Sunday Morning Monody

Faith is waiting in a queue
outside the Uffizi, one of two
ready to advance on cue
from the officials poised to shoo
and shoehorn twenty more in. Do
I dare enter without you,
my clued-up guide, without a clue?
Giotto, Duccio, Cimabue -
which Madonna is by who?
So was there some malentendu,
our date an *ombra* that *mai fu*?
No ticks confirm my text got through.
Forgive me if I misconstrue
a certain sense of déjà-vu,
but I was here when the cock crew,
waiting faithful in the queue.

La Chiesa di Dante

Enter, feigning nonchalance, the French tour
group to hear *Dominum Jesum Christum*
escape the newly christened sound system.
They amassed like it was 1034.
Electric candles. My eyes swept the floor,
my head hung penitent that her renown
should have reached me only through Dan Brown,
a Ser Brunetto counting his *tresor*.
Pre-Raphaelite-lite canvasses were browsed
where Beatrice and Dante were espoused
with the de' Bardi, the Donati. On
a lectern that served as a doorstop
parallel text invited me not
to abandon every hope but leave a small donation.

Valentine's Card, Venezia Nuova

They tear our tickets. The programmes
bear Goldoni's coat-of-arms,
librettoless, cast only.
Up here in the Gods I want
to make a paper aeroplane of mine,
scratch the fuselage with lines like these ones
and send it tailing over the stalls down your way.

It would contain our programme for the night,
the one bar in Livorno open even
though it's Friday, the date
we definitely haven't thought about.
At intervals I smile and brush
the ushers off, drop circles,
thank the stars outside you smoke.

A Vinanelle

I cherished once a red that now I rue.
You need to ask me why I look so glum?
It's all been thrown away on a ragù.

One year old, must mature another two
Before you can know the notes of violet, plum
And cherry in the red that I now rue.

Why couldn't Dionysus and his crew
Have parachuted in and stopped my Mum
From throwing it all away on a ragù,

Or at the very least have brought a brew
That savoured something of comfort's crumb?
I cherished once a red that I now rue,

Clutching the bottle and its residue.
And OK, I admit they salvaged some -
Not all was thrown away on the ragù -

But what does it matter when the cork was due
Another fourteen months under my thumb?
I cherished once a red that now I rue.
It's all been thrown away on a ragù.

The Vineyard

We sit down in the coming yield
and it half-shelters us. Not that
we need shelter: the sky is clean,
the moon quiet and alone just

above. Your lips are deeply sealed

until an item of forbidden fruit
undoes them, seed and skin
buried in the half-light of our trust.

The Icon

Una figura della donna mia

An image of my lady lives inside
The church of San Michele, where her grace,
Her holiness and loveliness provide
Asylum seekers with a safer space.
Thus she, when people kneedrop and draw near,
Prioritises those who need her most:
A milky retina turns crystal clear,
A demon is evicted from its host.
Her features clarified by candlelight,
Her name is on the lips of anyone
Aware how many patients she puts right
And leaves how many gobsmacked lookers-on
   Whom the Franciscans call idolaters
   While only dreaming of a crowd like hers.

- from the Italian of Guido Cavalcanti

Contradictions

Io vidi già seder nell'arme irato

I've seen a man-at-arms who oft succumbs
to white hot rage that none can pacify:
it even brings saltwater to his eye,
heart-boiled in his valves and atriums.
And lovers I have witnessed whose pain numbs
them into quiet, without a tear or sigh,
and people starving to the point that, try
as they might, no repast gets past their gums.
Regarding sails, I've watched them breast the swell
then gales submerge them, ragged and forlorn,
and though she was odds-on to win the race
I've seen a greyhound overshoot the chase.
As such forces of nature are we born,
with which excessive will does not go well.

- from the Italian of Leon Battista Alberti

The Wells

We've never got our water from the mains
but from a spring a few miles up the Law.
Makes bugger all difference when it rains
to the five households that have become four
since the blackguard neighbour we are feuding
with sank a borehole when the pressure slacked.
My Dad explained, admiring, grudging, brooding:
'Dig deep enough and water will collect.'

So when I'm under Medici Riccardi in
the stables of Lorenzo the Magnificent
and Virgilio says those wells
were dry when they found them, the sumping's recent,
I think of C_____ mocking our Edwardian
supply with his backyard harrowing of hell.

Boxes

She's stacked them outside the door,
so her new housemate
can move in this very
afternoon with a minimum of fuss.
Unlikely it's to spare

me the sight of the room, the mattress
where you woke to a smile never seen
so bright so early
and made yours truly yours
in body and soul, stripped bare.

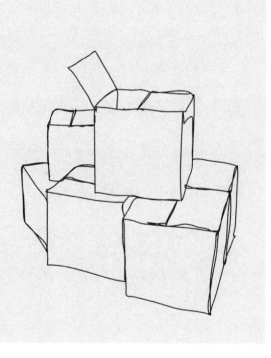

Three poems from Gaspara Stampa

A' che signor affaticar in vano

Why do they persist, lord, in their mission
to capture you in marble or on parchment -
trailblazing Michelangelo and Titian,
and other leading lights in those departments -

when I've engraved your image and defined
it so clearly on every quarter of my heart
and in every corner of my mind
that it survives us being separated?

Because, perhaps, you like to be portrayed
dependable, considerate, a gent,
as you are to everyone, in every way;

whereas, sadly - it hurts me to remind you -
you're stamped on me exactly as I find you:
a touch susceptible and arrogant.

Quando talvolta il mio soverchio ardore

When the consumptive agony exceeds
what human beings can reasonably sustain
I consider that these hands might turn on
myself and do a hurt to end all hurts,

but Love always pre-empts me with choice words
over my shoulder, his favoured lectern:
'Will you swing your scythe in another's grain?
Whatever right you had is now your Lord's

and has been ever since the day I gave
him you, in life and death, body and soul,
autonomous and wilful as a slave.

So if you, to you, were to bid farewell
and take yourself away without his leave,
it would be more than was forgiveable.'

Mentre, signore, alle alte cose intento

I know your mind is fixed on higher things
and that you have your honour to enhance:
no resting on your laurels won in France
like those which valorous Roman temples ringed,

not while I increase the salt content
of the Adriatic, this love-weighed-down
body dissolving into the main
until I see Death coming, and consent.

It's just that, because your every success
is trumpeted so far and wide, deafening
even the Italian peninsular,

in France they're not receiving these distress
signals which routinely move the heavens
and have never squeezed a tear out of you.

A Song from Padania

Each night I dream of going south
for hearts meridian are warm
where farmhands battle daily drouth
and every evening brings a storm.
Each night I dream of going south,
for hearts meridian are warm

where farmhands battle daily drouth
and every evening brings a storm,
where architecture's less uncouth
and Norman ramparts are the norm.
Each night I dream of going south,
for hearts meridian are warm.

Where architecture's less uncouth
and Norman ramparts are the norm,
'kisses from a female mouth'
land like a calabroni swarm
each night. I dream of going south,
for hearts meridian are warm.

Etna

for J. H. Cochrane

A lump of basalt from the underworld
is on my desk, a lightweight paperweight
from the moment the Mongibello unfurled
new tephra. It was touch and go underfoot
for walking boots broken in in Troutbeck.
Blast in the oven before it passed to me,
palm-warm as when you plucked it newly struck
off the lame god's anvil, the undersea
shelf-smelter, world-beater. Now you're gone,
the myth's expanded through your wife and son
to include the hairy bus journey
up the south flank where the driver put on
excerpts from *Norma*, the gentle Sicilian's
bel canto cracking over the tannoy.

Up At The Villa

The stitching tight in Europe's scars,
they get out of their motorcars
and scan the Tuscan sky for stars.

Wine mulling over their cigars,
they wonder how these Christmas trees
compare with Bloomsbury's Christmas trees.

With glimpses of the Bright Young Things
they hang up the old baubles, old tinselling,
savants and grand-daughters of kings.

Phase One

after Andrew Marvell

Had we but Disney+, on Prime
And Netflix we would spend less time.
We would lie back, unscroll our way
Through new releases, and hit play;
Then with end credits rolling, trade
Affairs of the heart, club, diamond, spade.
We'd Go Fish, Scopa, try The Ten,
Whose tricks are tallied by the pen
That lists our thoughts of daily bread,
Transcribing stomach more than head.

But at my back I always hear
The car emblazoned *polizia*,
And I'm afraid lest they should park it
To find my closest supermarket
Lies half a quartiere behind
Me and my dog-eared, dated, signed
Autocertificazione
Is out of date as panettone.

I see the story thus unwinding,
Me either being fined or finding
Myself a lodger in the clink
With nothing red or white to drink,
Regretting every step I had
The best of reasons not to add.

Carnevale MMXX

This farewell to the flesh they're taking
seriously, even the wags
in plague doctor masks. No one's aping
Byron who drained himself to the dregs.

Ordinances will this cold grey day
come into force. Let's refuel
on *risotto al nero di*
seppia, spread like an oil spill.

The Florence Duck Store

I want a hero, and shall call him Edison,
   A name one finds from Britain to Brazil,
For multiculturalism is a medicine
   To remedy not all, but many an ill.
We'll try; should it transpire that he has led us on
   A wild goose chase, may he fear my quill.
At this point, one should call upon the Muses;
But now I have my hero, I'll just use his.

Bassoonist with effective monoglossia,
   He'd come to spend a summer month in Florence,
Not being the only one to leave the mossier
   Meridians: they turned up in their torrents,
But few of them to understand what *ossia*
   Or *gaudioso* mean. I think he warrants
Applause for wanting to inspect the germs
Of meaning under the melodic terms.

Now, at the bottom of the Via della
   Vigna Nuova, or Street of the New Vine,
There is a rather specialistic toyseller
   Whose wares are nothing if not anatrine.
It's staffed by a *ragazza molto bella*
   Who spends most of her working hours online,
As you would, if a flock of ducks so tame
Was all the company that you could claim.

I wrote down 'flock', but now I doubt myself.
    I find such niceties a little addling,
But flocks are on the wing and not the shelf;
    A grounded group of ducks would be a 'badling',
Says Google, be it Ghibelline or Guelf
    Ground; when afloat, however, they're a 'paddling'.
We can dispense with badling, paddling, flock;
In this case, let's agree that they were stock.

Because every curious collective noun,
    The pride and glory of the English tongue,
Would raise a less infuriated frown
    Than the other mystery that dwelt among
Those shelves like a *bête noire* (or maybe brown):
    Namely, of what strange substance were they wrung?
We talk of rubber ducks, and ducks of plastic,
But realise the word 'rubber' is elastic.

But less attention's owed to their material
    Than to the various ways they were attired.
Some sported British uniforms imperial,
    And one or two were obviously inspired
By Queen Victoria, while the funereal
    Habiliments that Lincoln never tired
Of clothed another; though it's unclear whether
The beard was meant to be of hair or feather.

In vestments even blacker was the Sith
　　Lord nobody can fail to recognise,
Who shared a window with his boyish kith
　　And kin, the junior walker of the skies.
Lucasian, yes, but also Nordic myth
　　Dressed many other tempting bathroom buys,
Or not a single shelf would have been filled as
They were with Bayreuth-billing-worth Brünnhildes.

My better judgement tells me to curtail
　　This list, lest I attempt a technoscopic
Survey of every duck and drake for sale,
　　And get back to the fundamental topic
Of our protagonist, so young and hale.
　　From now on may the Muse remain myopic
And treat those jaundiced rubber tykes as scenery
Or, if they're lucky, narrative machinery.

Think of the comic plays of Aristophanes:
　　Animals almost always formed the Chorus,
Like wasps or frogs or storks, and made cacophonies
　　That would have drowned out a tyrannosaurus
Or even got a praying anchoress off her knees,
　　Had either been around in Epidaurus
When long gone was the giant theropod
And Christ was twinkling in the eye of God.

Edison passed the Duck Store every day,
  Because his room across the Ponte Carraia
Made Vigna Nuova the ideal way
  To reach the place where his linguistic fire
Was struck beneath a pedagogic ray.
  With a modicum of Latin to reacquire,
He learned that learning's easier when a nation's
Ceased declining, though kept the conjugations.

He looked in through the window every morning,
  And every morning he was flabbergasted
By the beauty - however much prior warning
  He gave himself - of the movie star miscasted
As this bespectacled commessa yawning,
  Texting - it didn't matter what the lass did:
How was it that she could behind a till be
More beautiful than any was or will be?

He always left his lodgings in good time,
  So found time one June morning, long before
The sun had hit his brutalising prime,
  To find himself immobile by the door,
Whose step seemed like an Everestal climb.
  Base camp avails nothing, though; therefore
He stepped into that realm of quiet quackery,
And saw more ducks than there are leaves in Thackeray.

Do not imagine this an idle reference,
  For she was studying a glossy *Vanity*
Fair (*Vogue*'s my all-things-being-equal preference,
  But both of them contribute to humanity) -
I mean the magazine, but show due deference
  To William Makepeace' novel and the urbanity
Of my uncle, who as a student read
It in a single spin of Earth, he said.

She looked up from her article, and smiled
  At Edison a smile that reduced
Him to the verbal power of a child
  Of three or four years, mobile or papoosed.
Who cares that he was meek as she was mild,
  That her features would confound the pen of Proust?
For they had reassumed their former solemn
Aspect and turned back to a glossy column.

Attractive though the ducks were just to browse, he
  Decided not to add to those who breeze
In and breeze out, or she would see a lousy
  Tight-fisted scrimper like a Genoese,
Conclusions which his line in foreign frowsy
  Did nothing to dispel. He gave a squeeze
To one, bequiffed and big and based on Elvis,
And hoped the waterline remained the pelvis.

He took this in one hand and then with both
    Placed it upon the desk, as if presenting
Her with a gift all people should be loath
    To accept, like an invitation tenting.
Its verisimilitude to the waisty growth
    Of the original was unrelenting,
But any comment on similitude,
Veri- or peri-, he reckoned rather crude.

His overtures, then, came out as soft susurri,
    As nervous, asyntactical white noise
Composed in a half-premeditated hurry.
    This never would have knocked the public poise
Of someone from a private school in Surrey,
    But having broken bread with different boys
He'd passed up opportunities to render
Himself more fluent with the other gender.

With every word he said, he wished them fewer,
    As we all wish all swarming summer creatures.
Barbaric though they must have sounded to her,
    Though, no pained reflex twitched across her features
As her language was bedraggled through the sewer
    With the names, had she but known them, of his teachers.
I planned to publish them, but then foresaw suits
Getting fat off the ensuing lawsuits.

Regaining then the pavement, he had reason
　　To feel his efforts hadn't come to nought,
Because she'd spoken gently in the season
　　Of sweet sighs, yes, but also tempers short.
But being more cheerful than the average Pisan
　　Hardly qualifies as a glowing report:
Just head downstream from Tuscany's largest flower
And mouths will turn as pendant as the tower.

He wanted nothing more than more occasions
　　To see her, learn about her, and displace
His legioned rivals; sadly, the equation's
　　Less simple than appears to be the case.
With three weeks left in Florence, no evasions
　　Of chances to familiarise his face
To her were possible, but suppose he got a
Reputation with her as a mere squatter?

His following purchase was a Pavarotti,
　　His white tie bursting with his bellowing.
Imagine if they'd manufactured Scotty
　　Moore's mantlepiece companion to the King!
But it appears that vocalists were what he
　　Desired, though this was an unconscious thing.
And as she scanned Luciano she surprised him
With a smile that implied she recognised him.

By 'him' I speak of Edison: the tenor
Could hardly fail to be identified.
He bought the overalled form of Ayrton Senna
The day after the next, whose subject died
A stone's throw from the city of Ravenna
(where I once used to happily reside),
And hoped the model of a man who raced
Time's wingèd chariot wasn't in bad taste.

Some Florentines (not her) rebuked his habit
Of being profligate with thanks and gratitude,
Which I put down, however dull and drab it
May seem, to differences in cultural attitude.
He still professed them like a headlit rabbit,
But had from her a comprehending latitude,
For if they try, one can't begrudge non-natives
Who don't know their accusatives from datives.

If only she had work as a barista,
Each conversation would have cost him less: oh,
Compared to these, he would have made at least a
Ninety-percent saving with espresso.
It's as unusual as a warm South-Easter,
Frequenting cafés daily; duck stores less so.
He couldn't just walk in and chat, for shame,
When she had never even asked his name.

She'd never put to him a question, now
  I come to think of it: she was content
To nod her head, incline it, and allow
  That he had said precisely what he meant
Unless it underscored a lifted brow,
  Which signalled that he wanted her dissent.
And when she granted it, he knew the knowledge
Would outlive what he learned in any college.

His days in Florence left to him were numbered;
  In euros he was down to his last twenty.
The only thing increased was what encumbered
  His bedside table: what they really meant he
Could not say, but they watched him while he slumbered
  And dreamed dreams of their retailer aplenty.
Who needs the base necessity of eating?
His final note would buy another meeting.

Next morning, he again propelled the door
  That had become familiar as his own,
And found himself transfixed there by a more
  Translucent smile than he had ever known.
'Since you're the loyallest patron of this store'
  She said, 'Take this. Keep it; it's not a loan.'
Unlike the others in his new flotilla,
This duck was classic, yellow, plain vanilla.

Arriving home, he noticed it was not
   The same as all the other ducks he'd shopped.
This one had a cutaway dorsal slot,
   And underneath a plug of some sort stopped
The threat of water entry, cold or hot.
He prised this with his fingernails: it popped,
He rummaged and, locating something there,
Pulled out a piece of paper, folded square.

This is, as you can see, a moneybox.
   I'm giving it to you so you cease squandering
Your liquid assets on our plastic flocks.
   Because I don't want you to go home wondering,
Longing to stop, indeed turn back the clocks,
   I have to let you know that someone's conned a ring
Onto my finger, namely my ring finger,
And even as I write, it seems to linger.

That someone, special someone, works out back,
   So if I haven't had so much to say
Don't diagnose it as a simple lack
   Of care or interest that I can't convey.
Perhaps you'd like to know we have a stack
   Of surplus, so if you can find a way
Tomorrow, or the day after tomorrow,
Leave time for me to steal, beg or borrow.

The Vineyard

Friction between the sheets
of cloud that roll offshore.
A storm is brewing. Our
skins ferment in the heat.

In a perfect silence
Etruscan gods take
their angers out on chalk.
A time to keep silence

unsplit by gigajoule
as black roosters sleep.
Our every pore drip
feeds gulping soil.

High Praise

Novelle ti so dire, odi, Nerone

Nerone, have you heard the whisperings?
It's going around you're actually quite hard,
And all attempts at comfort just help lard
Bondelmonti brows and other things.
They'd sooner tread upon a wyvern's wings
Than meet that resting bitchface, your trump card,
Stonier than any body's body-guard
Save Pharaoh's in the Valley of the Kings.
I can't approve of how you want to hound
Such noble blood from Florence, hoping they'll
Drop everything and leave it here for you.
And yet they did forget your debt, it's true:
More windfall for your soul's salvation fund.
It seems to work, this haggling tooth and nail.

- from the Italian of Guido Cavalcanti

In July

Receive this gift of peaches, Conad's finest, only to
apprise me of their many misapplications

from fruitbowl to bedside sickbucket to a picnic
for Pratolino's thoraxed legions

and tool in the Timothée Chalamet technique.
Pity the poor peaches and whom they've been through.

From Dante's Purgatorio XXVI

'Now you have some idea of why we're here.
Perhaps you'd like to know us all by name,
but there's not the time. Besides, I couldn't say,

so I'll fill you in on the essentials.
I'm Guido Guinizelli, one of those
who came clean and become clean.'

I heard and said nothing else. I just walked
alongside, admiration keeping me
more at arm's length than the fire could.

Then, when I had had enough of gawping,
I bowed before him, self-effaced,
and probably said something quite embarrassing.

And he replied: 'If my ears don't deceive me
any more than you do, even Lethe
won't be able to wash this memory.

But how do I know you're being genuine?
How do I know this isn't just an act
your guides and poet-friends are complicit in?'

And I to him: 'As long as our new language
is being used, those sweet, smooth poems of yours
will make the ink they're written in seem precious.'

'Oh no no no no...you see that one
I'm pointing at?' (I followed his finger)
'In his tongue, he was the better craftsman.

He could turn his hand to verse or prose,
romances, ballades, albas. I know some
champion the cretin from Limoges,

but they subscribe to fashion, not the truth:
and the truth is that a writer's reputation
depends on who's writing the reviews.

Anyway, if you have the chance to enter
the eternal court and everlasting hall
where Peter is the porter and Christ master,

say me a paternoster once you're in.
It'll make my time go a few grains faster
in this place, where we can no longer sin.'

And then, perhaps to make way for someone else,
he disappeared back into the flames
like a fish flashing down the water's edge.

The figure he'd pointed out was up ahead.
I caught up with him and asked him his name,
so I could write it down when I got home.

In his transalpine patois he replied:
So gratifying is that request you frame,
there's little I should want to hide from you.

I am Arnaut, and I walk and weep and sing.
I look back and see every little death.
I look forward to the life that's beckoning.

Just do me this, in the name of the One
Who decided that you would climb this stair.
When the time comes round, think about my pain.

He stepped back into the fire that made him better.

About the author

Harry Cochrane is a writer and journalist based in Florence, Italy, where he writes for *The Florentine* and the *Times Literary Supplement*. He was born in 1994 in Northumberland, UK.

With thanks to:

Susie & Alistair Cochrane, George Cochrane,
Judith Cochrane, Janet & Peter Harding,
Aimelie Moen, Elliott Park, Daria Chernysheva,
Daniel Shipley, Charlotte Chorley, Simon Gfeller,
Alexis Mountcastle, Mark Wormald,
Robin Kirkpatrick, Keith Sykes,
Ambrogio Camozzi Pistoja, Alan Jenkins,
Camille Ralphs, Helen Farrell, Leo Cardini,
Marco Badiani, Nico Mann and a great many great
others.

F THE LORENTINE / Press

Florence, February 2021

Printed in Great Britain
by Amazon

62973881R00031